How to Create Language Experts With
Literary Terms

Codi Hrouda and Emma McInerney
with Lyle Lee Jenkins

My Book of Prefixes and Suffixes

By: _____

School: _____

Teacher: _____

Date: _____

My Book of Antonyms

By: _____

School: _____

Teacher: _____

Date: _____

My Book of the "W" Questions

By: _____

School: _____

Teacher: _____

Date: _____

My Book of Author's Purposes

By: _____

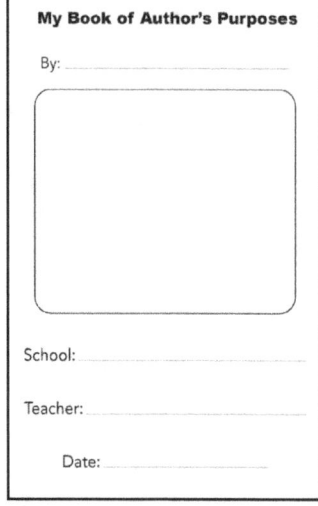

School: _____

Teacher: _____

Date: _____

My Book of Lessons Learned

By: _____

School: _____

Teacher: _____

Date: _____

Perfect School Collection™

To contact the authors regarding keynotes, workshops or bulk orders, visit LtoJ.net/Contact

ISBN: 978-1-956457-67-4

Book Design & Graphics: Christy Courtright, Christy's Customs LLC
Quality Assurance Manager: Kelly Lippert
Publishing Consultant: Martha Bullen, Bullen Publishing Services
Distribution Coordinator: Maggie McLaughlin

Printed in the United States of America

The Perfect School Collection™

How to Create a Perfect School by Lyle Lee Jenkins
How to Create a Perfect Home School by Lyle Lee Jenkins and Kelly Hawkinson Lippert

Perfect School Collection™ Resources

How to Create Math Experts series by Peggy McLean and Lyle Lee Jenkins
How to Create Math Experts with Fluency Quizzes by Peggy McLean and Lyle Lee Jenkins
How to Create Math Experts with Math Standards Quizzes by Peggy McLean, Laura Hayes and Lyle Lee Jenkins
How to Create a Math Foundation for Future Math Experts by Lyle Lee Jenkins
How to Create Bible Experts: Genesis to Revelation by Richard Douglas Junior Jenkins with Lyle Lee Jenkins

Early Readers

Bible Patterns for Young Readers series by Lyle Lee Jenkins
Aesop Patterns for Young Readers series by Lyle Lee Jenkins

Young Authors

Wordless Books for Young Authors series by Jim Chansler and Lyle Lee Jenkins

Special Project

All About Henry: Rich Widower of Savannah Valley by Lyle Lee Jenkins

CONTENTS

Purchasers of *How to Create Language Experts with Literary Terms* may utilize the QR code provided at the end of the book to download student booklets from this book at no extra cost. Both the print and downloaded copies are protected by copyright laws.

INTRODUCTION

The philosophy behind these booklets is that they are student-led, and elementary (K - 6) standards driven. In other words, students can independently complete much of the materials they are expected to learn in school with occasional pre-teaching.

The booklets are designed with a left-brain/right-brain balance. The back cover is a right-brain activity and the inside pages are clearly left-brain. The page prior to each grade level gives parents and teachers background knowledge and suggestions to successfully support their students and children through the booklets.

In order to create and assemble the booklets, parents and teachers can scan the QR code provided at the end of the book to download digital copies. To ensure proper printing, please utilize double sided printing and set your printer to "flip" on the short edge. The front page will be the front and back cover of the booklet. We have also included some bonus booklets within this series to support additional literary term exploration.

Enjoy,

Codi Hrouda, Emma McInerney and Lyle Lee Jenkins

GRADE 2
BOOKLET DIRECTIONS

My Book of Compound Words:
Students may need to be pre-taught what compound words are and given examples. Access to books that contain compound words will be needed for this booklet.

My Book of Prefixes and Suffixes:
Students may need to be pre-taught what prefixes and suffixes are and given examples. Access to books that contain prefixes and suffixes may be needed for this booklet.

My Book of Synonyms:
Students may need to be pre-taught what synonyms are and given examples. Access to their favorite books and song titles will be needed for this booklet.

My Book of Antonyms:
Students may need to be pre-taught what antonyms are and given examples. Access to their favorite books and song titles will be needed for this booklet.

My Book of Problems and Solutions:
Students will need to have access to fiction books.

My Book of the "W" Questions:
Students may need to be pre-taught the "W" questions (who, what, when, where and why), and why they are important for comprehension. Access to fiction books will be needed for this booklet.

My Book of Cultures That are the Same and Different:
Access to fiction books with similar plots with different cultural perspectives will be needed for this booklet. Students may need help interviewing a friend about their favorite holiday.

Some books we suggest:
Cinderella By Disney Book Group and *The Rough-Face Girl* by Rafe Martin
Goldilocks and the Three Bears By: James Marshall and *Goldy Luck and the Three Pandas* by Natasha Yim

My Book of Author's Purpose:
Students may need to be pre-taught on the ways authors write (persuade, inform, entertain). Access to books that are written for three different authors' purposes will be needed fr this booklet.

My Book of Lessons Learned:
Students will need to have access to fiction books.

List as many compound words as you can think of:

My Book of Compound Words

By: _____

School: _____

Teacher: _____

Date: _____

Fill in the blank to create a compound word:

_____ball

_____light

cross_____

_____body

water_____

fire_____

While reading a book, list any compound words you find:

Find or create words that have BOTH
a prefix and a suffix:

_____ _____

_____ _____

_____ _____

_____ _____

_____ _____

_____ _____

_____ _____

My Book of Prefixes and Suffixes

By: _____

School: _____

Teacher: _____

Date: _____

Use the definitions to fill in the correct prefix
for each word:

re - again
pre - before
un - not

_____school   _____fair

_____turn   _____pare

_____able   _____common

Circle the words where two or more prefixes
can be used:

cook   dress   warm

do   lock   aware

Rewrite each word using the correct suffix.
*Remember some base words may need to be changed

-s / -es - more than one

fox   book

_____   _____

worry   way

_____   _____

Fill in the blank with the correct word using -ed or -ing
-ed - happen<u>ed</u> in the past
-ing - happen<u>ing</u> now

The rabbit _____ in the yard.
        (hop)

My mom is _____ about the storm.
        (worry)

The man _____ to the police.
        (lie)

Student booklets are available via the QR code at the end of the book

Create a list of your favorite book titles.
Recreate parts of the title using synonyms

Book Title	New Title
_____	_____
_____	_____
_____	_____
_____	_____
_____	_____
_____	_____

My Book of Synonyms

By: _____

School: _____

Teacher: _____

Date: _____

Match words that are synonyms

Synonyms - words that have the same meaning

laugh   hurt

harm   mistakes

center   giggle

error   middle

love   adore

Rewrite the sentences using the synonym of the underlined word.

My grandma is <u>wealthy</u>.

_____

Susan is a good <u>pal</u>.

_____

I was very <u>tardy</u> to school.

_____

The bad <u>odor</u> is coming from the sacks.

_____

Student booklets are available via the QR code at the end of the book

Create a list of your favorite song titles.
Recreate parts of the title using antonyms.

Song Title | New Title

_____ _____

_____ _____

_____ _____

_____ _____

_____ _____

_____ _____

My Book of Antonyms

By: _____

School: _____

Teacher: _____

Date: _____

Match words that are antonyms.

Antonyms - words that have the opposite meaning

cold   odd

true   subtract

happy   hot

add   sad

even   false

Rewrite the sentences using the antonym of the underlined word.

Today, it is <u>cold</u> outside.

_____

The teacher asked the boy to <u>add</u> the numbers.

_____

The boat was <u>sinking</u>.

_____

She <u>smiled</u> at him.

_____

Student booklets are available via the QR code at the end of the book

Read a book and identify the problem and solution.
Create a new solution to the problem.

My Book of Problems and Solutions

Problem:

By: _____

Solution:

School: _____

New Solution:

Teacher: _____

Date: _____

Read two books. While reading, write down the character's main problem.
After reading, describe how the character solved the problem.

_____
Title of Book One

_____
Title of Book Two

Problem:

Problem:

Solution:

Solution:

Read a book. Then create and answer
"W" questions about the book.

My Book of the "W" Questions

By: _____

School: _____

Teacher: _____

Date: _____

Read two books.
Answer the "W" questions below.

Book 1	Book 2
Who is the main character?	Who is the main character?
_____	_____
What is the problem in the story?	What is the problem in the story?
_____	_____
Where is the story taking place?	Where is the story taking place?
_____	_____
Why did the character have this problem?	Why did the character have this problem?
_____	_____

Compare the way your family celebrates your
favorite holiday to the way a friend celebrates
their favorite.
(You may need to interview a friend to do this)

<u>My holiday</u>

<u>Same</u>

<u>Friends Holiday</u>

**My Book of Cultures That are
the Same and Different**

By: _____

School: _____

Teacher: _____

Date: _____

Read two books that are similar.
Then complete the diagram showing their similarities and differences of cultures.

<u>Book 1</u>

<u>Similar</u>

<u>Book 2</u>

Student booklets are available via the QR code at the end of the book

List titles of texts that have more than one author's purpose.

....

....

....

....

My Book of Author's Purposes

By: _____

[ ]

School: _____

Teacher: _____

Date: _____

Authors write for different purposes. Below are three purposes that authors use. Choose words from the word bank below that match each purpose

Dictionary   Fairytales   Advertisements

Comics   Biography   Opinion Piece

Persuade - the author tries to get you to do something or believe them.

....

Inform - the author gives you information about a topic

....

Entertain - the author tells a story that the reader will enjoy through pictures or words.

....

Read a book that matches each of the author's purposes below. Write the title and explain why it matches the author's purpose.

Persuade: _____
(title)

_____

....

Inform: _____
(title)

_____

....

Entertain: _____
(title)

....

....

Read a book and write the lessons learned. Describe a time you learned a similar lesson (your connection)

Lesson from your book:

_____

_____

_____

Your connection:

_____

_____

_____

My Book of Lessons Learned

By: _____

┌─────────────────────────┐
│   │
│   │
│   │
│   │
│   │
└─────────────────────────┘

School: _____

Teacher: _____

Date: _____

Read the short texts below. Tell the lesson learned.

1. Diego decided to stay up late on a school night to watch his favorite movie. The next day he found himself falling asleep. When he woke up, he figured out he missed the ending to the story being read aloud that he couldn't wait to hear. What lesson did Diego learn?

_____

_____

_____

1. Lisa's mom asked her to clean her room before her friends came over. Lisa decided to shove everything under her bed instead of putting things where they belong. When her friends came over, one of them reached for a game under the bed. Her friend saw the mess and Lisa became embarrassed. What lesson did Lisa learn?

_____

_____

_____

Read two books and write the lesson the character learned.

_____
Title of Book One

Lesson learned: _____

_____

_____

_____
Title of Book Two

Lesson learned: _____

_____

_____

CONTINUE CREATING LITERARY EXPERTS

BONUS BOOKLETS

A quick internet search for literary terms brings up hundreds of words. In addition, there are many topics to study as students gain more meaning from language and increase their writing skills.

Thus, the following blank pages are designed for students to write additional booklets about literary terms not included in *How to Create Language Experts with Literary Terms*. After selecting a new term, students select the format that best fits the task of writing about the literary term or concept.

There are times when children become so engrossed with a particular term that they want to make their booklet larger. These blank pages can also be used to add to existing booklets included in *How to Create Language Experts with Literary Terms*.

Student booklets are available via the QR code at the end of the book

My Book of _____

By: _____

School: _____

Teacher: _____

Date: _____

_____
Title of Book 1

_____
Title of Book 2

_____

_____

_____

_____

_____

_____

_____

_____

_____

_____

Student booklets are available via the QR code at the end of the book

My art:

Student booklets are available via the QR code at the end of the book

Book 1 Title: _____   Book 2 Title: _____

Book Title   Book Title

Student booklets are available via the QR code at the end of the book

Read two books and compare and contrast a literary element
(characters, setting, conflict, plot, and theme)

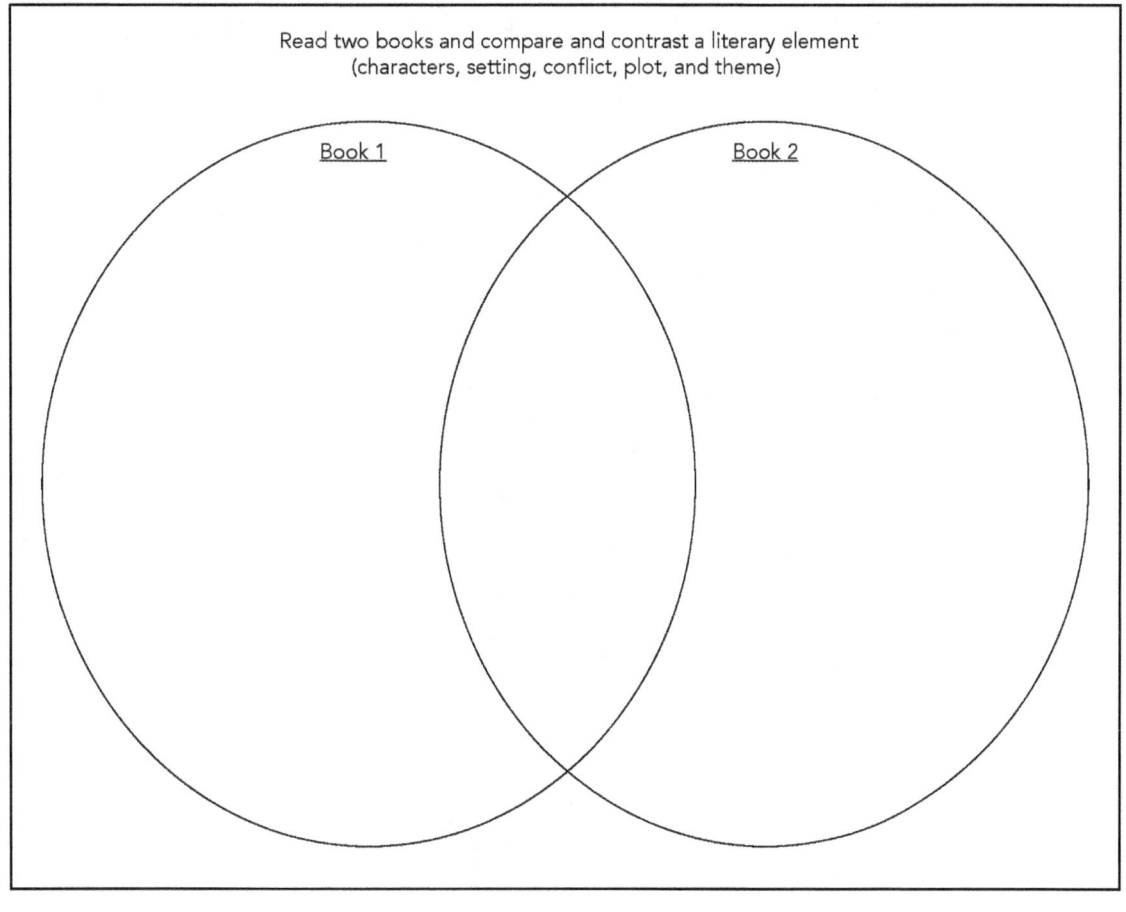

Book 1

Book 2

Student booklets are available via the QR code at the end of the book

_____
Book Title

_____
Book Title

_____
Title of Book One

_____
Title of Book Two

Student booklets are available via the QR code at the end of the book

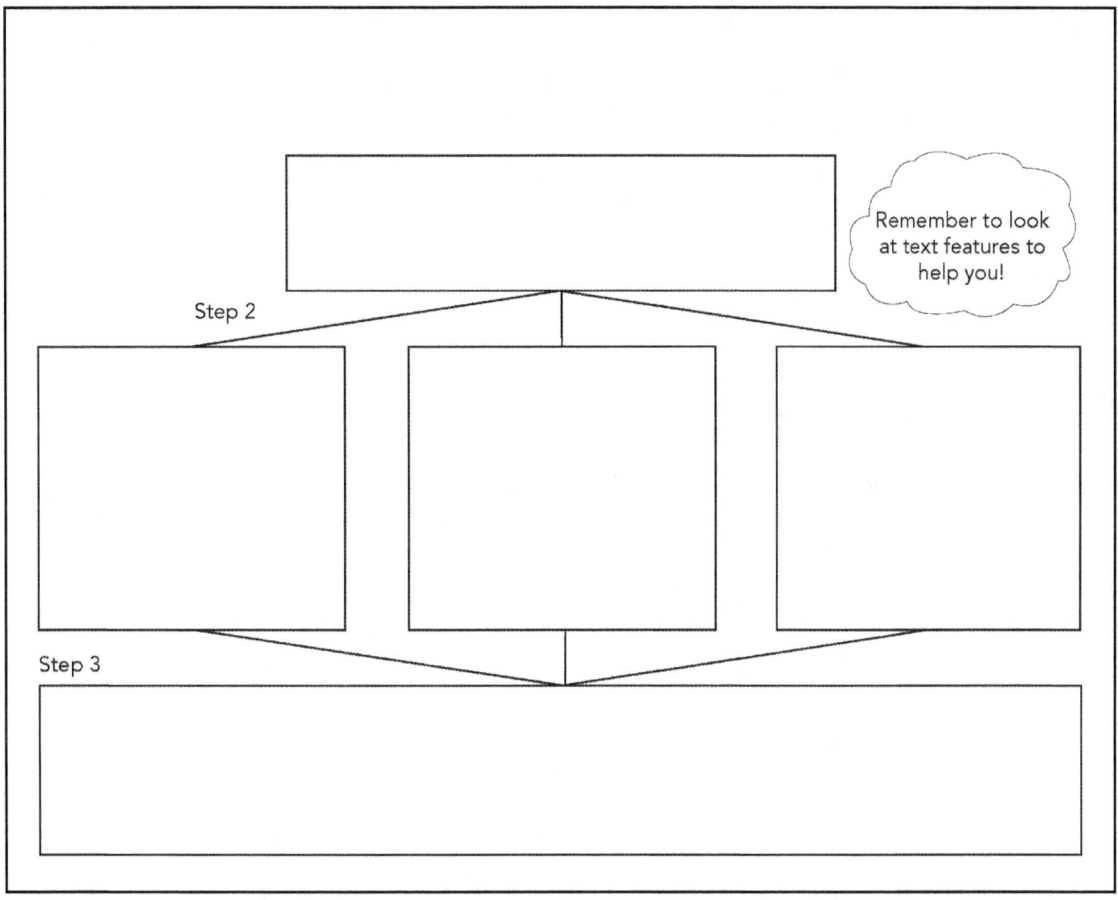

Step 2

Remember to look at text features to help you!

Step 3

Student booklets are available via the QR code at the end of the book

STUDENT BOOKLET
DOWNLOAD

Purchasers of **How to Create Language Experts with Literary Terms** may use this QR code to download booklets from this book at no extra cost. This will ease the process of making copies for students and expand learning options. Both the print and digital download versions of this material are protected by copyright laws.

QR codes can be found in all LtoJ books, providing access to digital downloads of student worksheets.

ABOUT THE AUTHORS

Codi Hrouda grew up in the small town of Hubbard, Nebraska. After completing high school, Codi went on to pursue her degree in Elementary Education at Wayne State College, and graduated with a BA in Elementary Education in 2000.

Once graduated, Codi accepted her first job at Thurston Elementary School, in Thurston, Nebraska, as a fifth and sixth grade combination teacher. A year later, she and her husband moved to Columbus, Nebraska where she taught a year of first grade and then thirteen years of fourth grade at Centennial Elementary School. While teaching full-time in Columbus, she completed her master's degree in Curriculum and Instruction through Wayne State College. She graduated with her master's degree in May of 2006.

In 2014, Codi and her husband moved their family back to the area where she grew up to raise their three daughters. Codi accepted a fifth grade position at Dakota City Elementary in Dakota City, Nebraska where she continues to teach today. She just completed her twenty-second year of teaching in 2022. Codi spends her free time attending her daughters' activities, decorating, reading, and spending time with her family and friends.

Emma McInerney grew up in the small town of Elk Point, South Dakota. After completing high school, Emma went on to pursue a degree in healthcare at South Dakota State University (SDSU).

In 2015, she realized she was ready for a career change because her passion lies in education. She transferred to Dakota State University (DSU), earned a degree in Elementary Education, and graduated in 2019. Emma began her first job at Dakota City Elementary, in Dakota City, Nebraska, as a fifth grade teacher. While teaching full-time she completed her Masters degree in Curriculum and Instruction through Wayne State College, graduating in May of 2022. Emma concluded her third year of teaching in 2022, and she continues to teach alongside her co-author, Codi Hrouda.

Emma returned to her hometown of Elk Point after graduating, and spends her free time reading, gardening, and spending time with her boyfriend, family, and friends.

Dr. Lyle Lee Jenkins is an author, speaker, and recognized authority in improving educational outcomes. He believes that implementing a growth mindset and celebrating progress are the keys to helping students learn more and retain their enthusiasm for school.

His education experience, that spans over 50 years, ranges from working as a teacher, a principal, and a school superintendent in the California School System to being a University Professor. In 2003, Lyle Lee founded LtoJ, LLC hoping to impact and guide the way we approach education.

Lyle Lee Jenkins has authored six books showcasing continuous improvement in schools, including *How to Create a Perfect School*, *Optimize Your School*, *Permission to Forget*, *From Systems Thinking to Systemic Action*, *Improving Student Learning*, and *How to Create a Perfect Home School*. All literature offers powerful, practical suggestions for every aspect of education. The two most influential people supporting Dr. Jenkins's work are W. Edwards Deming and John Hattie.

Having spoken to educators all across the United States, Latin America, Europe, Australia, and Asia, Lyle Lee Jenkins is passionate about equipping the next generation with a true love of learning.

Dr. Lyle Lee Jenkins holds a Bachelor of Arts degree from Point Loma Nazarene University, a Masters of Education from San Jose State University and a Ph.D. from the Claremont Graduate University.

Lyle Lee Jenkins's website, www.LtoJ.net, is a great place to discover useful tools to guide your educational journey.

Do you have a great photo or video of your student using one of our products?

We would love the opportunity to share it on our website and social media channels!

Email us at info@ltoj.net

If you have a story to share, we would also like to hear from you. We feature student stories during presentations and on our social media accounts.

Our team loves sharing the joy of a child understanding new concepts. It allows our audience to experience firsthand the mission our team works towards every day; for students to maintain the same love of learning they brought to Kindergarten throughout all their years of schooling and into adulthood.

Thank you for being a loyal customer. We appreciate you!

The LtoJ Team

Follow us on Instagram, Facebook, TikTok and YouTube
@LtoJLLC